The Rockwool Foundation Research Unit

Serving time or serving the community? Exploiting a policy reform to assess the causal effects of community service on income, social benefit dependency and recidivism

Signe Hald Andersen

University Press of Southern Denmark
Odense 2012

Serving time or serving the community? Exploiting a policy reform to assess the causal effects of community service on income, social benefit dependency and recidivism

Study Paper No. 37

Published by:
© The Rockwool Foundation Research Unit and
University Press of Southern Denmark

Copying from this book is permitted only within
institutions that have agreements with CopyDan,
and only in accordance with the limitations laid
down in the agreement

Address:
The Rockwool Foundation Research Unit
Sølvgade 10
DK-1307 Copenhagen K

Telephone   +45 33 34 48 00

Fax   +45 33 34 48 99

E-mail   forskningsenheden@rff.dk

Home page   www.rff.dk

ISBN 978-87-90199-63-0
ISSN 0908-3979
January 2012
Print run: 350
Printed by   Specialtrykkeriet Viborg A/S

Price: 60.00 DKK, including 25% VAT

Contents

Abstract 5

Introduction 6

Community service in Denmark 7

    Why and how does imprisonment matter? 7

    Stigmatization 8

    Investments 8

    Harmful effects of community service? 9

    Identification strategy 10

    Instrumental variables approach or difference-in-difference estimation? . . 11

Data 13

    Variables 14

Results 17

    Results by offender type 21

    Bias caused by business cycles? 22

    Community service participants and offenders sent to prison 23

    Community service participants and a non-criminal comparison group . 24

Conclusion 26

References 27

Appendix 29

Serving time or serving the community? Exploiting a policy reform to assess the causal effects of community service on income, social benefit dependency and recidivism

Signe Hald Andersen

Abstract

There is a widespread belief among criminologists, judges and the like that criminals are better off serving non-custodial sentences instead of going to prison. However, empirical evidence of the effects of community service is scarce. This paper exploits a policy reform that implemented the use of community service as punishment among specific groups of criminals, Danish administrative data, and difference-in-difference matching in order to assess the causal effect of community service on post-sentence income, dependency on social benefits, and crime. The results show that community service participants have higher long-run income levels and lower long-run levels of social benefit dependency compared to offenders who serve custodial sentences. However, while community service lowers recidivism among offenders convicted of violent crime and misdemeanor, there are no overall effects of community service on crime committed after the serving of a sentence.

Introduction

The immediate purpose of placing offenders in prison is to punish their criminal activity. But it is widely recognized that the punishment does not end with release from jail, as several types of subsequent, informal sanctions trouble the lives of ex-prisoners. Studies show that ex-prisoners experience more unstable intimate relationships (e.g. Lopoo & Western, 2005), earn lower wages, and have a weaker labor market affiliation (e.g. Waldfogel, 1994; Western et al., 2001). However, these findings may reflect the effects of several factors related to the prison sentence – the selection of certain individuals into a criminal career, the impact of being convicted, the actual stay in prison, etc. This last possibility was discussed as early as the mid-19th century, when prominent criminologists such as Arnould Bonneville De Marsangy claimed that shorter prison terms in particular are harmful, as they are too short to facilitate rehabilitation, but long enough for the hardened criminals in the prison to contaminate the prisoner with their "criminality" (Villetaz et al., 2006; Killias & Villetaz, 2008). Thus, according to Bonneville de Marsangy, offenders would fare better if they could avoid prison.

Today, justice systems in most countries have different types of sentences at their disposal, including traditional imprisonment, suspended sentences, electronic monitoring and community service. The use of the non-conventional – or more specifically, the non-custodial – types of sentence is often due primarily to considerations of the increasing cost of keeping people in prison and of prison overcrowding, but as a more or less intentional side effect, offenders then also avoid the potential contamination encountered in jail. But while most judges, criminologists and the like still believe in Bonneville's claim, empirical evidence on the actual causal effect of non-custodial sentences is scarce. In an excellent review study published in 2006, Villetaz et al. show that at that time only five studies assess the causal effect of non-custodial sentences on post-sentencing outcomes. While some of these studies find positive effects of especially community services compared to traditional imprisonment, the review concludes that overall, there is no evidence of positive outcomes from non-custodial sentences. Recently Killias and colleagues published evidence from two controlled, randomized experiments that assess the causal effect of community service and electronic monitoring on different post-sentencing outcomes (Killias et al., 2010a; 2010b). While the first study (Killias et al. 2010a) finds no difference between community service and traditional custodial sentences, the finding of the second study (Killias et al. 2010b) suggests marginally significant differences between two types of non-custodial sanctions, electronic monitoring and community service, in favor of the former. However, the evidence is still relatively limited, particularly as most of the existing studies rely on rather small samples which may explain the frequent result that the effects found are non-significant. In effect, we need more knowledge on the harmful consequences of serving a custodial vs. a non-custodial sentence before we know whether Bonneville's assumption of contamination is correct.

This present study contributes to the existing literature on the causal effect of non-custodial sentences by exploiting a policy reform on the use of community service in Denmark. For this purpose, I analyze full-sample individual-level data using difference-in-difference matching, and analyze the effects of doing community service rather than serving a prison sentence on several short- and long-term post-sentence outcomes, including labor market outcomes and recidivism. The results indicate that community service participants earn more and are less dependent on social benefits in the long term, yet, there is no overall evidence of lower recidivism rates.

Community service in Denmark

While larger European countries such as Germany, Switzerland and the UK implemented community service in the 1970s, Denmark was more reluctant to initiate the use of this type of non-custodial sanction. But after a trial period, community service was introduced in January 1992.

Initially, community service could be used to replace prison sentences for specific types of crime, such as misdemeanor and less serious types of violent crime; however, in 2000 a reform was passed that allowed judges to also impose community service on drunk drivers and other types of traffic offenders. Today, community service can replace prison sentences for all types of crimes which would otherwise incur prison sentences of less than 12 months. However, judges are obliged to exercise a certain degree of caution and not to use community service in cases where a non-custodial sentence might offend the public's sense of justice (for instance, in cases of robbery or sexual crime).

In Denmark, community service comprises between 30 and 240 hours of work that contributes to society (e.g. in public libraries, kindergartens, community centers, etc.), and while many countries determine the number of hours of community service by the length of the non-custodial sentence it replaces, Danish law does not impose a direct scale of conversion. Instead, the judge decides on the appropriate length of the community service, given the offenders' different characteristics (Lagoni & Kyvsgaard, 2008). During the period of community service, the offender lives in his or her normal home, and keeps his or her job. In the following section, I discuss whether and how community service may leave the offender better off than traditional prison sentences.

Why and how does imprisonment matter?
One explicit purpose of imprisonment is to prevent recidivism by rehabilitating and restraining the offender. However, both scholars and practitioners seem to agree that the incarceration also has less attractive consequences that the use of non-custodial sentences such as community service may help to avoid (Schwartz

& Skolnick, 1962). The theoretical and empirical literature on the negative effects of incarceration identifies several explanations for the harmful effects of incarceration.

Stigmatization

One explanation emphasizes the stigmatization related to imprisonment. This is labeling theory. Here, a number of studies use experiments to demonstrate significant discrimination against job applicants with criminal records. By varying only the criminal history of otherwise identical applicants, the studies demonstrate employers' reluctance to hire ex-offenders, even for positions that do not require the holder to have a clean record (Schwartz & Skolnick, 1962; Cohen & Nisbett, 1997; Pager 2003). These findings very well reflect the effects of stigmas, which are defined by Goffman as "blemishes of individual character perceived as weak will, domineering or unnatural passions, treacherous and rigid beliefs, and dishonesty, these being inferred from a known record of, for example, mental disorder, imprisonment, addiction, alcoholism, homosexuality, unemployment, suicidal attempts, and radical political behavior" (Goffman, 1963: 3). Thus, in the absence of full knowledge of an individual – in this case, the applicant – the people with whom the individual comes into contact (e.g. potential employers) extrapolate from the obtained knowledge of the criminal record to unobserved individual characteristics. This image may or may not correctly describe the individual, but demonstrates the common perception of ex-offenders that prolongs their informal punishment indefinitely. According to labeling theory, the stigma of incarceration may also work through the prisoners' acceptance of this deviant image given to them by their social relations (Lemert, 1972).

While offenders who serve both custodial and non-custodial sentences are likely to suffer from the stigma of having a criminal record, we may reasonably assume that society makes a harsher judgment of offenders who have been in jail: Society is likely to perceive a prison stay as a stronger marker of a bad personality than a non-custodial sentence. Interestingly, this perception is partially supported by the advice judges get not to use community service where it may injure the public sense of justice (as mentioned earlier), which is a strong signal that more serious offenders should serve their sentences in prison. As a result, ex-offenders who served non-custodial sentences may experience less stigmatization than ex-offenders who served custodial sentences (Western et al., 2001).

Investments

A second explanation emphasizes how incarceration affects human capital by allowing prison inmates fewer years at the ordinary labor market. This is likely to erode their job skills and restrict their possibilities of acquiring experience (Western et al. 2001; Waldfogel, 1994). This mechanism may not only apply to labor market experience, but could also affect the offender's possibilities of "investing" in other social relations, such as friendships and marriage, that could have promoted positive outcomes both at the labor market and in other domains (Hagan, 1993; Lopoo & Western, 2005; Sampson & Laub, 1993). Thus, if ex-offenders have worse outcomes than others, it may be that their unstable affiliation with normal society prevents them from making continuous investments in relationships. However, serving a non-custodial sentence will reduce offenders' absence from society, which suggests that ex-offenders who serve a non-custodial sentence may have better outcomes than ex-offenders who serve custodial sentences.

It is possible to think of additional reasons why custodial sentences might be more harmful than non-custodial sentences. A prison term may accelerate the onset of mental illness, for example, or may promote friendships with delinquent peers (an explanation similar to Bonneville's concern over contamination). Both these are processes that are likely to negatively affect outcomes after serving a prison sentence.

Harmful effects of community service?

But while the literature presents several explanations for the effects of incarceration, we may also speculate as to whether a community service sentence is simply a traditional sentence without the prison element, or whether this type of non-custodial sentence involves other potentially useful or harmful elements that affect post-sentence outcomes. For instance, whereas conventional custodial sentences facilitate a separation between offenders' criminal sphere and their other spheres (e.g. legal work and family life), community service will confuse these spheres, as the offender now serves his or her sentence while at the same time acting as an active member of a family and an active employee. Consequently, the non-criminal sphere is no longer unaffiliated with the offender's criminal life, and this may impair the use of the non-criminal sphere as a lever to encourage desistance after the sentence has been served (see, for example, Sorensen & Kyvsgaard, 2009). Serving a sentence as community service may then impede desistance from crime among this group of offenders. In addition, one aim of imprisonment is to deter present and future offenders from committing (further) crime (Gorecki, 1979; Gibbs, 1988), and this deterrence is lacking from, or at least reduced in, community service. As a result, community service participants may not fully realize the implications of their wrongdoings, and consequently be less likely to desist from crime after the sentence. This is the specific deterrence theory as described by Wilson (1983; see also Windzio, 2006).

Thus, while we may be able to think of several negative consequences of serving a prison sentence that result primarily from impairment of the offender's reputation and social and human capital, community service may also be far from ideal and cause negative outcomes by affecting individual processes of desistance. In sum, we may expect negative outcomes for both offenders sentenced to imprisonment and offenders sentenced to community service; however, the common perception is that imprisonment leaves the offender worse off than community service. To identify the causal effect of participating in community service on various labor market outcomes and on recidivism, I exploit the implementation of the community service scheme in Denmark, as described below.

Identification strategy

Despite the introduction of community service in 1992, Danish judges displayed an initial and protracted reluctance to use this non-custodial sentence. However, with the reform in 2000, the use of community service accelerated, particularly for the punishment of offenders of misdemeanor, simple violence, drunk driving and other traffic offenses. Figure 1 shows the use of community service between 1990 and 2009. The figure demonstrates a doubling between 1999 and 2001 in the number of misdemeanor and violent crime offenders who were sentenced to community service. It also shows how the number of drunk drivers and other traffic offenders who received a community service sentence rose from zero to 1,500 and 500 per year respectively over the same period, which was a direct effect of the reform.

Figure 1: The use of community service, different types of offenses, 1990-2009.

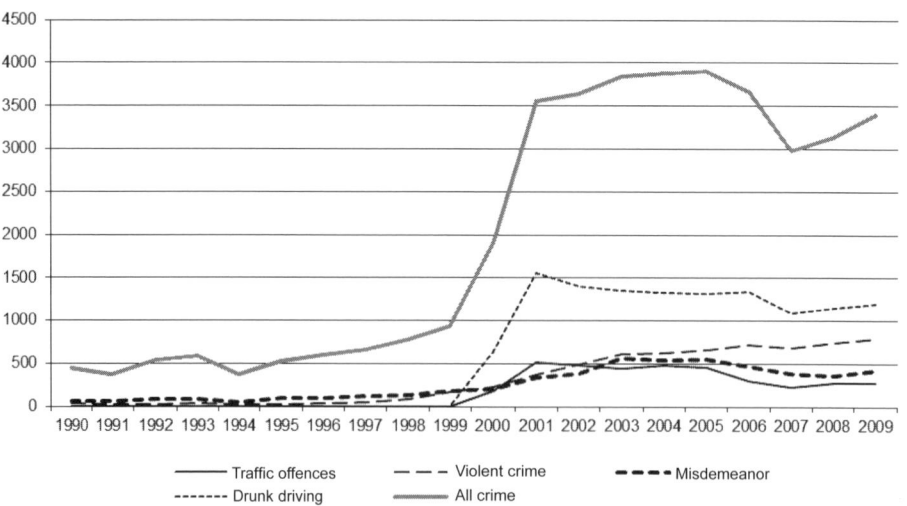

Source: Own calculations based on data from Statistics Denmark

Today, approximately 2/3 of all offenders who commit crimes that would trigger prison sentences of up to 12 months are actually imprisoned, and 1/3 are sentenced to doing community service. Obviously allocation to one or the other type of sentence does not happen at random: Allocation into community service relies on the judge's assessment of the offender's suitability for this type of sentence. This implies that differences after completion of sentences between the offenders who are sent to jail and offenders who are sentenced to community service are likely to reflect the initial differences that determine their type of sentence rather than a causal effect of how they served their sentence. If, for instance, offenders sentenced to community service are more likely to have a job at the time of the conviction – since having a job may make the judge assume that the offender is more likely to complete the community service – this characteristic is also likely to increase the probability that offenders in this group will still hold a job after finishing the sentence. This would then cause differences in, for example, the post-sentence income and unemployment of imprisoned offenders and offenders doing community service that would only be spuriously related to the type of sentence. Rather, such differences would reflect the initial selection criterion used by the judge. As a result, one cannot arrive at a causal estimate of the effect of community service compared to traditional imprisonment just by comparing the outcomes for the two groups, as the allocation of offenders into sentence types is endogenously related to the different outcomes. However, with the right empirical strategy, the observed changes in the use of community service shown in Figure 1 can be used to facilitate causal inference.

Instrumental variables approach or difference-in-difference estimation?

As is evident from Figure 1, an offender's probability of being assigned to community service rather than traditional imprisonment is strongly correlated with year of conviction. Thus even if type of sentencing is correlated with individual characteristics across these years, the dramatic increase in the use of community service from 1999 to 2001, will push a relatively large group of offenders – that is, those at the margin – from traditional imprisonment into community service. This shift represents an exogenous change in the probability of being sentenced to community service that reflects the reform, and the shift is uncorrelated with the individual characteristics of the offenders at the margin. If we assume that average offender characteristics do not change over the period covered by the figure, the implementation of community service would represent a natural experiment that we may exploit for making causal inference in an instrumental variables (IV) model (Wooldridge, 2002; Greene, 2003). However, this assumption is not fulfilled in my sample, as offenders who are convicted in different years differ with regard to several observed – and probably also unobserved – background characteristics (results not shown). Thus, even though the presence of a reform makes IV estimation an obvious choice, this strategy is not possible with my sample.

Another useful strategy is to employ the difference-in-difference estimator. This estimator represents a state-of-the-art approach to causal inference, as it eliminates all observed and unobserved time-invariant differences by comparing differences between treatment and control groups in changes in social benefit dependency, wages and crime rates before (t-1) and after (t+1) the offenders served their sentences. Equation 1 explains the procedure. Here, $\overline{Y}_{t-1}$ is the pre-treatment outcomes and $\overline{Y}_{t+1}$ the post-treatment outcomes. T and C signify the treatment status (T are the treated and C are the controls).

$$[1] \quad \hat{d}_D = (\overline{Y}^T_{t+1} - \overline{Y}^T_{t-1}) - (\overline{Y}^C_{t+1} - \overline{Y}^C_{t-1})$$

The difference-in-difference model does solve many of the problems related to making causal inference, but is, however, sensitive to differences in time trends between the treated and the controls. This could be a problem if one wants to assess, for example, the treatment effect on recidivism when the treated and the controls are not the same age (due to selection bias in treatment status). In such a case, we would find the two groups at different points on the age-crime curve, which means that the "natural" slope of their criminal activities differs, whereby also their post conviction outcomes will differ, not due to their sentence type, but due to these initial differences. I solve this problem by reframing the difference-in-difference setup as a matching estimator, where I match my samples of treated and controls on a range of background characteristics, including thorough controls for previous crime, income and dependency (i.e. $\overline{Y}_{t-r'}$, where r' signifies any period prior to the treatment date). My outcome is $\overline{Y}_{t+r}$ (r signifies any period after the treatment date), and provided that my samples are adequately matched on $\overline{Y}_{t-r'}$, my results – the difference between the treated and controls for $\overline{Y}_{t+r}$ – is a treatment effect that has the same properties as $\hat{d}_D$, but which also balances the samples with respect to time trends prior to the treatment. This estimator produces unbiased results if the distribution of the unobserved individual specific components that affect selection into treatment and subsequent outcomes is similar across the matched treated and controls (Chabé-Ferret, 2010). In some cases, this may be a strong and unrealistic assumption; however, the procedure I use for selecting the treated and the controls is likely to meet the conditions necessary for that assumption to be valid. I use kernel matching, but test whether my results are robust to other matching algorithms.

Data

In Denmark all residents have a unique personal number which identifies them in a great many transactions, such as submission of tax forms, interaction with the welfare system, schooling, registration of work status, and registration of residence. Statistics Denmark collects the information annually, and makes these data available – in anonymous form – for statistical and research purposes. The available data constitute a panel that goes back as far as 1980 and currently ends in 2009. The data provide information on each resident's criminal behavior – e.g. information on offense dates, reasons for charges, conviction dates, and type of sentence – and also on income and a range of background characteristics. We obtain information on dependency rate from DREAM, an administrative database run by the Ministry of Employment, which provides weekly information on benefit receipts in Denmark. While the data from Statistics Denmark also contain this information, the DREAM database contains the most recent information on individual-level receipt of benefits.

From this data, I choose a sample of individuals who have been convicted of one of the offenses that judges most frequently punish with community service. These are drunk driving, misdemeanor (e.g shoplifting and vandalism), violent crime and other traffic offenses. To obtain a suitable sample, I first delimit the sample to those who have been sentenced to either community service or prison. Community service is intended to be a substitute for imprisonment, and not for other types of sentence, which makes individuals sentenced to prison the appropriate control group to compare with the group of community service participants. Second, I delete individuals sent to prison who received sentences of longer than a year – community service only replaces prison sentences shorter than a year.

Third, I delimit the sample to include only those who were sent to prison in 1999 and those who were sentenced to community service in 2001. This is to arrive at as accurate a control group as possible that will fulfill the assumptions of my model (as described earlier): Individuals who were sentenced to prison in 2001, when the community service option was available, are likely to be poor matches to community service participants convicted in 2001, and will thus not have the same distribution of individual-specific unobserved characteristics as those who were sentenced to community service. However, in contrast, we are likely to find perfect matches among the individuals sentenced to prison in 1999, when community service was not an option.

Fourth, I drop individuals who both served a prison sentence and did community service during the three-year period 1999-2001. These individuals would belong to both the treatment and the control groups, and this makes it difficult to include them in either group. Fifth, as Danish women do not commit much crime, I focus only on male offenders. Thus my final sample consists of 6,042 observations, 4,279 who were sentenced to prison in 1999 and 1,763 who were sentenced to community service in 2001. Given the selection criteria described above, the higher number of offenders sentenced to prison terms makes sense, as this group contains the smaller subgroup who would have gotten community service sentences had it been an option in 1999.

Importantly, with these definitions of treatment and control groups, changes in contextual differences – such as the business cycle – might affect differences in outcomes for the two groups, and thus bias the estimates. I test this by comparing the results to similar calculations based on the current control group of offenders who were sent to prison in 1999 and a treatment group of offenders sentenced to jail terms in 2001, and by adjusting for time trends observed in a group of non-criminal but otherwise comparable males.

Variables

As stated in the introduction, this paper assesses the short- and long-term effects of serving a community service sentence on three outcomes: social benefit dependency, wage income and crime. From the data I obtain information on weekly benefit dependency and wage income in the 2nd to the 5th years after the year of the conviction ($t+2$, $t+3$, $t+4$ and $t+5$), and on crime in the 2nd to the 4th years after the year of the conviction ($t+2$, $t+3$ and $t+4$). Note that social benefit dependency includes all types of unemployment benefit for insured and uninsured workers (including time spent in active labor market programs), early retirement pension, and sick leave benefits. Crime includes all convictions except traffic offenses. Note that I exclude traffic offenses as they are often not considered real crime in the literature.

Table 1 shows the distribution of these outcomes in the whole sample and in the sub-samples as specified by type of sentence. We see that community service participants have lower dependency rates during all the years considered. As we measure dependency by weeks, the differences are not trivial, as they amount to almost 5 weeks during the first year (26.46-21.81= 4.65), and to more than 9 weeks (29.61-20.07=9.54) during the last year ($t+5$). Second, and in line with the higher dependency rates, the community service participants earn more in all the years of measurement. The difference in, for example, $t+5$ is 5.09, corresponding to DKK 50,900 (EUR 6,787). Again, these differences are non-trivial. Third, the community service participants commit less crime after their convictions than the imprisoned offenders (I measure crime as the number of recorded convictions).

As discussed earlier, my matching setup is meant to resemble a difference-in-difference approach, where results reflect the change in outcomes caused by the treatment (or, for the control group, the absence of the treatment). Consequently, a thorough control for pre-treatment outcomes, $\overline{Y}_{t-1}$, is essential. I therefore include values on pre-treatment outcomes measured at t-1, but also at t-2 and t-3, to account for time trends prior to the year of the conviction. Table 1 shows the descriptive statistics for these variables, and as can be seen – and as was expected – community service participants fare far better on these variables. They have lower dependency rates, higher incomes and lower crime rates.

The last section of Table 1 shows descriptive statistics for the controls. First, I include information on the type of crime committed (whether drunk driving, violence, misdemeanor or another type of traffic offense). I also control for the extent to which the offenders had been convicted of such crimes in the three years prior to the current conviction. I moreover control for age, marital status, number of children, and education (whether the offender has more education than elementary school). These are valid controls, as they are likely to signal information that the judge may take into account when deciding on sentence types. Again we see how the community service participants score better on these measures than the offenders sentenced to prison, as they are less likely to have been convicted of any of the four types of crime prior to the current offense, more of them have families, and they are better educated.

Table 1: Descriptive statistics

		All	Offenders sentenced to prison	Offenders sentenced to community service
Outcome variables				
Social benefit dependency				
	t+2	25.10 (22.11)	26.46 (21.93)	21.81 (22.19)
	t+3	25.76 (22.47)	27.11 (22.23)	22.56 (22.73)
	t+4	26.37 (22.62)	28.46 (22.38)	21.36 (22.43)
	t+5	26.81 (23.64)	29.61 (23.13)	20.07 (22.55)
Annual income from wages (x DKK 10,000)				
	t+2	10.54 (12.60)	9.71 (12.08)	12.55 (13.56)
	t+3	10.49 (12.56)	9.50 (12.15)	12.88 (13.19)
	t+4	10.16 (12.70)	8.88 (12.13)	13.26 (13.50)
	t+5	10.54 (13.09)	9.04 (12.42)	14.13 (13.91)
Crime				
	t+2	0.36 (0.77)	0.42 (0.84)	0.21 (0.56)
	t+3	0.34 (0.79)	0.40 (0.87)	0.20 (0.53)
	t+4	0.34 (0.80)	0.39 (0.86)	0.23 (0.64)
Pre-treatment outcomes				
Social benefit dependency				
	t-1	21.13 (21.34)	23.48 (21.54)	15.48 (19.76)
	t-2	20.19 (21.15)	22.62 (21.30)	14.32 (19.56)
	t-3	18.91 (20.97)	20.96 (21.16)	13.96 (19.66)
Annual income from wages (x DKK 10,000)				
	t-1	11.38 (12.33)	10.18 (11.83)	14.26 (13.02)
	t-2	10.98 (12.26)	9.78 (11.57)	13.86 (13.33)
	t-3	10.64 (11.99)	9.43 (11.49)	15.52 (12.66)
Crime				
	t-1	0.39 (0.83)	0.48 (0.91)	0.18 (0.49)
	t-2	0.42 (0.91)	0.52 (1.02)	0.19 (0.53)
	t-3	0.39 (0.87)	0.47 (0.97)	0.18 (0.50)
Controls				
Drunk driving				
	t	0.53 (0.50)	0.45 (0.50)	0.68 (0.47)
	t-1	0.04 (0.21)	0.04 (0.20)	0.05 (0.22)
	t-2	0.06 (0.24)	0.06 (0.24)	0.06 (0.24)
	t-3	0.05 (0.23)	0.05 (0.22)	0.06 (0.24)

Violence				
	t	0.31 (0.46)	0.38 (0.48)	0.16 (0.37)
	t-1	0.03 (0.18)	0.03 (0.19)	0.02 (0.16)
	t-2	0.05 (0.24)	0.06 (0.27)	0.02 (0.16)
	t-3	0.04 (0.22)	0.05 (0.25)	0.01 (0.12)
Misdemeanor				
	t	0.12 (0.33)	0.14 (0.35)	0.09 (0.28)
	t-1	0.06 (0.26)	0.07 (0.28)	0.03 (0.19)
	t-2	0.06 (0.29)	0.08 (0.33)	0.02 (0.13)
	t-3	0.05 (0.26)	0.06 (0.28)	0.03 (0.18)
Other traffic offenses				
	t	0.04 (0.20)	0.03 (0.16)	0.07 (0.26)
	t-1	0.11 (0.37)	0.11 (0.38)	0.10 (0.34)
	t-2	0.10 (0.35)	0.11 (0.37)	0.08 (0.30)
	t-3	0.10 (0.35)	0.10 (0.37)	0.08 (0.31)
Age		33.20 (11.45)	32.65 (11.05)	34.52 (12.26)
Single		0.64 (0.48)	0.66 (0.47)	0.58 (0.49)
No. of children		0.46 (0.91)	0.44 (0.90)	0.50 (0.93)
More than elementary school		0.37 (0.48)	0.35 (0.48)	0.44 (0.50)

Source: Own calculations based on data from Statistics Denmark

Results

Table 2 shows the results from the propensity score model – note that this is similar across outcomes, as the treatment remains the same, regardless of whether we focus on social benefit dependency, income or crime as our outcome.

The results presented in Table 2 are not surprising, as they describe the same pattern as we saw in Table 1. Community service participants have more resources than imprisoned offenders, and they are younger. Interestingly, of the variables that measure pre-treatment outcomes (benefit dependency, income and crime), not all are significant. This could be an indication of correlations between the variables measured at t-1, t-2 and t-3. However, I retain all the variables in the model in order to ensure proper balancing of the two samples, particularly with regard to time trends prior to conviction. The results also reveal that compared to the drunk drivers, offenders convicted of misdemeanor and violent crimes are less likely to be sentenced to community service, while other traffic offenders are no more likely to receive this sentence. Note also that the R^2 of this model is relatively high, which suggests that the model manages to reasonably account for the allocation into sentence type.

Table 2: Results from the propensity score model.

Control variables		Coefficient
Pre-treatment outcomes		
Social benefit dependency		
	t-1	-0.003 (0.002)
	t-2	-0.008 (0.002)***
	t-3	-0.000 (0.002)
Annual income from wages (x DKK 10,000)		
	t-1	-0.000 (0.003)
	t-2	-0.007 (0.004)
	t-3	0.007 (0.003)**
Crime		
	t-1	-0.295 (0.046)***
	t-2	-0.066 (0.041)
	t-3	-0.137 (0.044)**
Controls		
Drunk driving		
	t-1	0.265 (0.097)**
	t-2	-0.020 (0.084)
	t-3	0.119 (0.088)
Violence		
	t	-0.626 (0.050)***
	t-1	0.405 (0.116)***
	t-2	-0.135 (0.107)
	t-3	-0.193 (0.125)
Misdemeanor		
	t	-0.279 (0.066)***
	t-1	0.282 (0.099)***
	t-2	-0.260 (0.114)**
	t-3	0.141 (0.103)
Other traffic offenses		
	t	0.271 (0.086)***
	t-1	0.051 (0.052)***
	t-2	-0.095 (0.057)
	t-3	-0.068 (0.055)
Age		-0.004 (0.002)**
Single		-0.085 (0.044)
No. of children		-0.003 (0.023)
More than elementary school		-0.002 (0.040)
	Intercept	0.223 (0.110)**
	Chi²	743.41***
	Pseudo R²	0.1022

***: p<0.001; **: p<0.01: *: p<0.05
Source: Own calculations based on data from Statistics Denmark

Table 3 shows the results from the matching. Columns with the headings "treated" and "controls" show average levels of benefit dependency, income and crime for each group at t+2, t+3 t+4 and t+5. In the column headed "Diff." a positive coefficient indicates a positive treatment effect and a negative coefficient indicates a negative treatment effect. Note that the balancing properties of the model are quite good, as the Chi^2-value is low and the R^2 is tiny. Table A1 in the appendix shows the balancing of the two samples – of treated and controls – with regard to the background characteristics included. It is again evident that the samples are well-matched, as there are no significant differences between them.

From the table we learn that community service participants have significantly lower dependency rates in the long term. The differences are quite high, and vary between nearly 2.5 and 5 weeks. Moreover, community service participants also have higher earnings than offenders who serve in prison, but the differences are only significant in the long term. However, at this point they are non-trivial, as the coefficient of 2.19 corresponds to DKK 21,900 (EUR 2,920) – recall that the average annual income at t-1 is approximately DKK 113,800 (EUR 15,173), which amounts to a treatment effect of almost 20 percent.

Last, community service participants commit fewer crimes in the first two years after the sentence, but same amount of crimes in the last year. Importantly, these differences are not significant.

On the basis of these results, we thus find quite distinct positive long-term effects of community service on income and dependency. These results are not sensitive to choice of matching algorithm, as nearest-neighbor matching and 1:10 nearest-neighbor matching produce similar results (results not shown).

Table 3: Results from kernel matching

Social benefit dependency		Controls	Treated	Diff. (std.err.)
	t+2	21.03	21.84	0.81 (0.67)
	t+3	21.69	22.52	0.83 (0.68)
	t+4	23.71	21.26	-2.45 (0.68)**
	t+5	24.88	19.97	-4.90 (0.68)***
Annual income from wages (x DKK 10,000)				
	t+2	12.81	12.53	-0.29 (0.39)
	t+3	12.46	12.88	0.42 (0.39)
	t+4	11.76	13.28	1.52 (0.39)**
	t+5	11.94	14.13	2.19 (0.40)***
Crime				
	t+2	0.24	0.21	-0.03 (0.02)
	t+3	0.22	0.20	-0.02 (0.02)
	t+4	0.23	0.23	-0.00 (0.02)
Chi^2 for balancing			6.05	
Pseudo R^2 for balancing			0.001	

***: p<0.001; **: p<0.01; *: p<0.05
Source: Own calculations based on data from Statistics Denmark

20   Results

Figures 2, 3 and 4 show the results graphically. Here we see that the two groups – the control group, which consists of offenders sentenced to prison, and the treated group, which consists of offenders sentenced to community service – are very similar with regard to benefit dependency, income and criminal activity prior to their conviction (which is the result of the reform in combination with the matching). But we also see that they differ – in some cases significantly – after their conviction.

Figure 2: Social benefit dependency before and after conviction

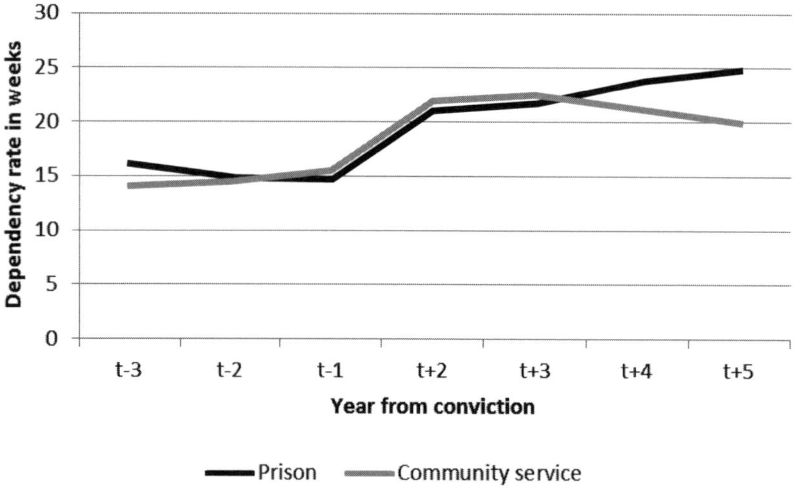

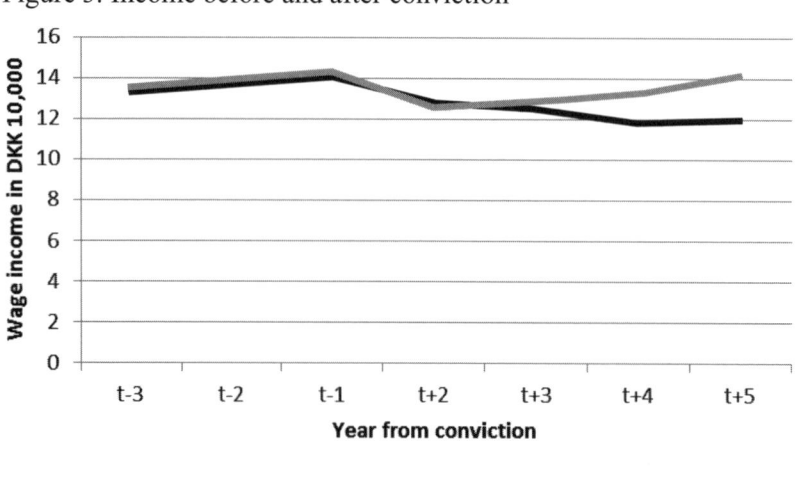

Source: Own calculations based on data from Statistics Denmark

Figure 3: Income before and after conviction

Source: Own calculations based on data from Statistics Denmark

Figure 4: Crime before and after conviction

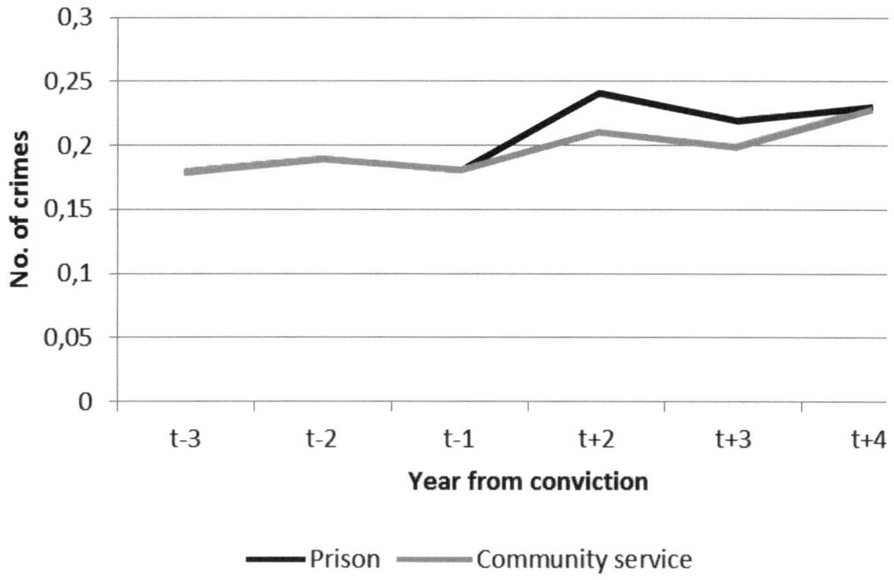

[Line chart showing No. of crimes on y-axis (0 to 0.3) against Year from conviction on x-axis (t-3, t-2, t-1, t+2, t+3, t+4). Two lines: Prison and Community service. Both start around 0.18 at t-3, remain flat until t-1, then rise. Prison rises to about 0.24 at t+2, dips to 0.22 at t+3, and ends at 0.23 at t+4. Community service rises to about 0.21 at t+2, dips to 0.20 at t+3, and ends at 0.23 at t+4.]

Source: Own calculations based on data from Statistics Denmark

Results by offender type

As mentioned earlier, my sample consists of four different types of offenders: drunk drivers, perpetrators of misdemeanor and violent crime, and other traffic offenders. As these types of crime are very diverse, and hence the offender groups are quite diverse, it is likely that the treatment effect – the effect of doing community service – differs among groups, meaning that each type of offender contributes differently to the overall effect. The results presented in Table 4 test this assumption by presenting results based on sub-samples defined by offender types.

These results show an interesting pattern, and it is evident that the four groups of offenders do indeed contribute differently to the overall conclusions. First, we find a negative effect of community service on short-term benefit dependency and income for drunk drivers. Second, the samples of drunk drivers and violent offenders drive the effect of community service on long-term benefit dependency. Third, we retrieve the long-term effect of community service on income in the sample of drunk drivers and violent offenders, and, to some extent, in the sample of misdemeanor offenders. However, the size of the coefficients varies remarkably between samples, and it seems that effects are strongest for offenders of misdemeanor, where the income difference between community service participants and offenders sentenced to prison is as much as DKK 28,300 (EUR 3,773) in the year t+4. Fourth, we find significant effects of community service on short-term crime among the violent and misdemeanor offenders. Among these groups, community service reduces recidivism by as much as 0.2 crimes in the short term.

Table 4: Results from kernel matching, by offender type

Outcome	Type of crime	Drunk driving	Misdemeanor	Violence	Other traffic offense
Social benefit dependency					
	t+2	2.26 (0.85)**	1.24 (2.25)	-3.15 (1.33)*	0.32 (2.81)
	t+3	1.94 (0.86)*	0.33 (2.29)	-1.87 (1.41)	0.33 (2.80)
	t+4	-1.94 (0.86)*	-2.16 (2.27)	-3.32 (1.40)*	-1.94 (2.97)
	t+5	-5.22 (0.87)***	-3.22 (2.36)	-4.40 (1.42)**	-1.09 (3.02)
Annual income from wages (x DKK 10,000)					
	t+2	-1.01 (0.47)*	1.27 (1.21)	0.61 (0.79)	0.07 (2.30)
	t+3	0.06 (0.49)	1.09 (1.26)	1.34 (0.82)	-0.11 (2.36)
	t+4	1.21 (0.49)*	2.83 (1.26)*	2.30 (0.84)**	-0.15 (2.45)
	t+5	1.92 (0.50)**	2.49 (1.33)	2.75 (0.89)**	0.47 (2.48)
Crime					
	t+2	-0.00 (0.02)	-0.07 (0.09)	-0.16 (0.05)**	0.03 (0.11)
	t+3	0.02 (0.02)	-0.21 (0.09)*	-0.09 (0.05)	-0.24 (0.13)
	t+4	0.01 (0.02)	-0.03 (0.12)	-0.06 (0.06)	0.09 (0.10)
Chi^2 in propensity model		107.79***	163.85***	211.60***	9.87
R^2 in propensity model		0.0259	0.2155	0.1365	0.0312
Chi^2 for balancing		2.63	2.02	2.05	0.97
Pseudo R^2 for balancing		0.001	0.005	0.003	0.003

***: $p<0.001$; **: $p<0.01$: *: $p<0.05$
Source: Own calculations based on data from Statistics Denmark

Bias caused by business cycles?

However, as mentioned earlier, my results may be biased by differences in, for example, the state of the business cycle experienced by the control group and the treatment group – the two groups were sentenced two years apart, and changes in the Danish economy in this period are likely to have affected both the dependency rates and the income options of the two groups. We know, for instance, that Denmark suffered from a small recession in 2003 and 2004, and this recession is likely to have affected our treatment effects. These changes will be disguised as part of the treatment effect, which will then be biased. I test this possibility in two ways.

First, I conduct an additional kernel matching with the same control group, but a treatment group consisting of offenders convicted of drunk driving, other traffic offenses, misdemeanor and violent crimes who were sentenced to imprisonment for less than a year in 2001. This treatment group is somewhat artificial, as its treatment does not differ from the treatment of the control group – both were sent to prison for the same offenses and for the same amount of time. However, the two groups are treated at times when the economic situation was different, and the effect of this "treatment" will give an indication of potential bias in my original estimates caused by the different economic situations. Thus, comparing the results from these analyses with my original results (presented in Table 3) will show if and how these original results are affected by time trends. Note, however, that such comparisons rely on the assumption that time trends affect the two groups equally.

In a second sensitivity analysis, I conduct a time trend adjustment of my original results using time trends in dependency rates, income and crime rates observed in the general population of Danish men. Under the assumption that these time trends are the same as the time trends of the population of community servers, this procedure should then cleanse the original results of these time trends.

Community service participants and offenders sent to prison

Table 5 shows the results of the first analysis, where I compare the original effects of community service presented in Table 3 with time trends for offenders sent to prison. The table shows whether the differences between the two sets of results are significant. We may interpret the size of the difference as the effect of community service, cleansed of potentially disturbing period effects.

As can be seen, there are some significant period effects, as offenders imprisoned in 1999 and 2001 differ, particularly with regard to their post-sentence dependency rates. These differences follow the same patterns as the differences observed for the community service participants. We also note a significant period effect with regard to income in t+3 – imprisoned offenders convicted in 2001 have lower income in t+3 than offenders convicted and sent to prison in 1999.

But in addition, the differences between the two sets of results – for community service participants and offenders sentenced to prison respectively – are significant for all outcomes. This first of all suggests a treatment effect of community service net of period effects. But the size of the difference also suggests that the period effect drives most of the effect of community service on short-term dependency, as only the long term effects of -1.79 respectively -2.80 (corresponding to 2 respectively 3 weeks) is large enough to actually matter. We also observe that while the effect of community service on income is positive (though insignificant), the effect of imprisonment in 2001 vs. imprisonment in 1999 is negative, suggesting that the effect of the community service is underestimated. Thus, our community service participants probably would have had significant positive gains from their non-custodial sentence also in the short run, had it not been for the negative time trend in income. The same is true for the last outcome, crime. Here, the period effect is positive – suggesting more recidivism – and this leaves us with an even larger negative and significant effect of community service.

Table 5: Comparison of treatment effects and period effects

Social benefit dependency		Community service participants	Offenders sentenced to prison	Diff. (std.err.)
	t+2	0.81 (0.67)	1.74 (0.61)**	-0.93 (0.01)***
	t+3	0.83 (0.68)	1.81 (0.62)**	-0.98 (0.01)***
	t+4	-2.45 (0.68)**	-0.66 (0.62)	-1.79 (0.01)***
	t+5	-4.90 (0.68)***	-2.10 (0.64)**	-2.80 (0.01)***
Annual income				
	t+2	-0.29 (0.39)	-1.10 (0.32)**	0.81 (0.01)***
	t+3	0.42 (0.39)	-0.73 (0.32)*	1.15 (0.01)***
	t+4	1.52 (0.39)**	0.80 (0.33)*	0.72 (0.01)***
	t+5	2.19 (0.40)***	1.24 (0.35)**	0.95 (0.01)***
Crime				
	t+2	-0.03 (0.02)	0.08 (0.03)**	-0.11 (0.00)***
	t+3	-0.02 (0.02)	0.06 (0.03)**	-0.08 (0.00)***
	t+4	-0.00 (0.02)	0.07 (0.03)**	-0.07 (0.00)***

***: p<0.001; **: p<0.01: *: p<0.05
Source: Own calculations based on data from Statistics Denmark

Community service participants and a non-criminal comparison group

In the second sensitivity analysis I rerun the original analysis using time trend corrected outcome and balancing measures. This is to test whether general time trends drive my conclusions. For this purpose I calculate mean income, dependency and crime rates in a group of Danish males for all relevant years and determine an index year (2000). I then use the ratio between the index year and year t to adjust outcome and balancing measures in year t in my original sample of offenders imprisoned in 1999 and offenders in community service in 2001. To the extent that the time trends in my original sample and in the general sample of Danish males are the same, this strategy should then produce results that are unbiased by time trends.

Table 6 shows the time trends adjusted results. As can be seen, the results do not change dramatically. I still get significant long run effects of community service on dependency rates and on income, however now, the insignificant short run effect have the same signs as the significant long run effects. In contrast to what we saw in the original results I now get a significant and negative short run effect of community service on crime. Thus to the extent that we can rely on the assumptions of this time trend correction, there is no reason to fear that the original results are severely biased by fluctuations in the business cycle.

Table 6: Time trend adjusted results

Social benefit dependency	Controls	Treated	Diff. (std.err.)
t+2	20.29	19.52	-0.77 (0.62)
t+3	19.87	19.35	-0.52 (0.61)
t+4	20.98	18.36	-2.63 (0.60)**
t+5	21.15	16.94	-4.21 (0.59)***
Annual income from wages (x DKK 10,000)			
t+2	12.51	13.22	0.71 (0.41)
t+3	12.80	13.35	0.55 (0.40)
t+4	12.27	13.49	1.23 (0.41)**
t+5	12.24	14.02	1.77 (0.41)**
Crime			
t+2	0.24	0.19	-0.04 (0.02)*
t+3	0.22	0.20	-0.03 (0.02)
t+4	0.22	0.23	0.00 (0.02)
Chi² for balancing			6.05
Pseudo R² for balancing			0.001

***: $p<0.001$; **: $p<0.01$: *: $p<0.05$
Source: Own calculations based on data from Statistics Denmark

Conclusion

The overall conclusion that we may derive from the analyses presented above is that the type of sentence that offenders serve – either custodial or non-custodial – does matter, as results consistently point to significant differences between offenders who are sentenced to imprisonment and offenders who participate in community service. Importantly, community service participants fare better with regard to long-term social benefit dependency and income, especially when we disregard the possible effects of time trends. In addition, offenders convicted of violent crimes and misdemeanor experience lower recidivism if they participate in community service.

The results presented in this paper relate to a specific change in the Danish penal system that happened in 2000. However, to the extent that the results have external validity beyond the population studied here, the ever-increasing incarceration rates in both Denmark and other countries, such as the US, should be a matter for concern. Since incarceration seems to reduce some offenders' possibilities of reentering and contributing to society, the ever-increasing use of imprisonment as a punishment for both more and less serious crimes will not only be costly throughout the duration of the sentence, and will prevent offenders from contributing directly to society during their imprisonment, but it will also be costly in the long run, in that imprisonment weakens the labor market affiliation of the former prisoners. In addition, to the extent that some offenders are more likely to commit further crime if they are imprisoned – as is evident for the group of violent offenders and offenders of misdemeanor – increasing incarceration rates will potentially lead to even higher incarceration rates in the future. This causes problems that not only pertain to financial issues and prison overcrowding; such increasing crime rates will also affect the overall well-being and productivity of society and its citizens. Thus, more initiatives like the extended use of community service and electronic monitoring would be highly useful.

References

Chabé-Ferret, Sylvain (2010): To Control or Not to Control? Bias of Simple Matching vs. Difference-In-Difference Matching in a Dynamic Framework. Found at http://www.cerdi.org/uploads/sfCmsNews/html/2782/Chabe_Ferret_26_nov_2010.pdf.

Cohen, Dov & Nisbett, Richard E. (1997): Field experiments Examining the Culture of Honor: The Role of Institutions in Perpetuating Norms about Violence. *Personality and Social Psychology Bulletin,* 23(11): 1188-1199.

Gibbs, Jack P. (1988): Toward Theories about Criminal Justice. *Journal of Contemporary Criminal Justice,* 4: 20-36.

Goffman, Ervin (1963): *Stigma: Notes on the management of spoiled identity.* Englewood Cliffs, NJ: Prentice Hall.

Gorecki, J (1979): *A theory of criminal justices.* New York. Columbia University Press.

Greene, W. H. (2003): *Econometric Analysis.* Prentice Hall: New Jersey.

Hagan, John (1993): The social embeddedness of crime and unemployment. *Criminology*, 31(4): 465-491.

Killias, Martin & Villetaz, Patrice (2008): The effects of custodial vs. non-custodial sanctions on reoffending: Lessons from a systematic review. *Psicothema*, 20(1): 29-34.

Killias, Martin, Gilliéron, Gwladys, Villard, Francoise & Poglia, Clara (2010a): How damaging is imprisonment in the long-term? A controlled experiment comparing long-term effects of community service and short custodial sentences on re-offending and social integration. *Journal of experimental Criminology*, 6: 115-130.

Killias, Martin, Gilliéron, Kissling, Izumi & Villettaz, Patrice (2010b): Community Service versus Electronic Monitoring – What Works Better? *British Journal of Criminology*, 50: 1155-1170.

Lagoni, Trine Møller & Kyvsgaard, Britta (2008): Forløb af samfundstjeneste. Justitsministeriets Forskningsenhed. Found at http://www.justitsministeriet.dk/fileadmin/downloads/Forskning_og_

dokumentation/forloeb_af_samfundstjeneste.pdf.

Lemert, E. (1972): *Human deviance, social problems and social control.* New Jersey: Prentice Hall.

Lopoo, Leonard M. & Western, Bruce (2005): Incarceration and the Formation and Stability of Marital Unions. *Journal of Marriage and Family*, 67(3): 721-734.

Pager, Devah (2003): The mark of a criminal record. *American Journal of Sociology*, 108: 937-975.

Sampson, Robert & Laub, John (1993): *Crime in the making. Pathways and turning points through life.* Cambrigde, MA: Harvard University Press.

Schwartz, Richard D. & Skolnick, Jerome H. (1962): Two Studies of Legal Stigma. *Social Problems,* 10(2): 133-142.

Sorensen, Dave & Kyvsgaard, Britta (2009): *Afsoning i hjemmet: En forløbsanalyse vedrørende fodlænkeordningen.* Justitsministeriets Forskningsenhed. Found at http://www.justitsministeriet.dk/fileadmin/downloads/ Forskning_og_dokumentation/Rapport_om_forlaenkeforloebet.pdf

Villettaz, Patrice, Killias, Martin & Zoder, Isabel (2006): *The Effects of Custodial vs. Non-Custodial Sentences on re-Offending: A Systematic Review of the State of Knowledge.* Campbell Systematic Reviews, 2006: 13.

Waldfogel, Joel (1994): The Effect of Criminal Conviction on Income and Trust "Reposed in the Workmen". *Journal of Human Resources,* 29(1): 62-81.

Western, Bruce, Kling, Jeffrey R., & Weiman, David F. (2001): The labor market consequences of incarceration. *Crime and Delinquency*, 47: 410-427.

Wilson, J. Q. (1983): *Thinking about crime,* revised edn. New York: Vintage Books.

Windzio, M. (2006): Is there a deterrent effect of pains of imprisonment? The impact of 'social costs' of first incarceration on the hazard rate of recidivism. *Punishment & Society*, 8: 341-64.

Wooldridge, Jeffrey M. (2002): *Econometric Analysis.* MIT Press: Cambridge.

Appendix

Table A1: Balancing properties of kernel matching

Control variables		% bias
Pre-treatment outcomes		
Dependency rate		
	t-1	-2.8
	t-2	-2.3
	t-3	-2.7
Annual income (x DKK 10,000)		
	t-1	1.8
	t-2	1.2
	t-3	1.9
Crime		
	t-1	0.6
	t-2	0.3
	t-3	-0.2
Controls		
Drunk driving		
	t-1	-0.7
	t-2	-1.4
	t-3	-1.1
Violence		
	t	-1.0
	t-1	0.3
	t-2	0.9
	t-3	1.2
Misdemeanor		
	t	0.6
	t-1	0.0
	t-2	1.0
	t-3	0.5
Other traffic offenses		
	t	5.5
	t-1	0.2
	t-2	-0.4
	t-3	-2.1
Age		-2.4
Single		0.0
No. of children		-0.8
More than elementary school		-0.6